THE PRIEST'S HANDBOOK

MORE WILDSIDE CLASSICS

THE PRIEST'S HANDBOOK

SECOND EDITION
Revised & Expanded

by
Bishop Karl Prüter

WILDSIDE PRESS

THE PRIEST'S HANDBOOK

This edition published in 2006 by Wildside Press, LLC.
www.wildsidepress.com

CONTENTS

CONTENTS

FOREWORD

Five years ago, when *The Priest's Handbook* was first published, I suggested that it should be called *A Provisional Priest's Handbook*, and asked for your suggestions so that I could write a new and better *Handbook*.

I want to thank the readers of that first *Handbook* for the many suggestions and criticisms which they have sent. Many, of course, dealt with the rules on funerals. It is appropriate to set down rules based on strict Scriptural teachings and sound theology, but many of our customs are governed by the culture from which we come. Although I stated that the priest must handle every funeral with great tact and compassion, some number of people were offended by the principles which were set forth.

We need, of course, to treat the bereaved compassionately and wherever possible to follow the customs and traditions of those involved, while at the same time we must protect the integrity of the Christian Faith.

Less serious were the criticisms regarding the rule that all weddings performed by Orthodox and Catholic priests must be celebrated in a Chapel, Church, or Cathedral. Garden weddings may seem suitable, but they do not witness to the faith which we profess when we unite couples in Christian union. A few wrote to say that they had had performed garden weddings, but upon further consideration had decided not to do so in the future. One reader tried to justify performing a wedding service on the baseball diamond. Perhaps he felt the rule of baseball that "three strikes and you're out" would reduce the amount of domestic violence. Or perhaps I just didn't understand.

In any case, I appreciate all your suggestions. I have given all of them earnest consideration in preparing this new edition. I trust you will also feel free to write to me concerning this Second Edition, so that in time, the Third may be better and cover some of the pastoral concerns that I may have overlooked.

+ Karl Prüter
Highlandville, Missouri

I.

THE RIGHTS AND DUTIES OF PASTORS

1. A priest must know that he serves because he has been called by Christ. It follows that his service is first to God and then to the people of God.

2. To help him in his service in God's Church, he has been placed under the authority of a bishop and the Holy Synod.

3. The bishop (ordinary) shall determine the assignment of each priest.

4. In all matters involving canon law, spiritual function, priestly rights and duties, the priest is under supervision of the bishop who is his ordinary.

5. A priest desiring a transfer from his parish must submit, in writing, a confidential petition to the bishop; such petition must be kept in confidence, but may be revealed to the Archbishop or Metropolitan. The bishop will determine whether a transfer should be made and if so, make a new assignment.

6. No priest has or shall claim any individual rights to ownership to the properties of his parish except as otherwise may be provided by contract.

7. No priest may enter into any contractual agreements, or otherwise engage in any business enterprise, which by its nature may jeopardize the assets of his

parish, or may subject such parish to any claim, lawsuit, or other liability arising from such activity.

8. No priest shall purchase any vestments that are to be charged to his account. Purchase of all and any church goods must be paid for at the time of purchase.

9. Every priest, active or retired, must have a telephone in his home with a listed telephone number. Exceptions in unusual circumstances can only be made with the permission of the bishop.

10. A priest, when asked what church he serves, must clearly state what jurisdiction he serves, and as best as he is able, make certain that the questioner understands whether he is Catholic or Orthodox. If Catholic, it must be clear that he is not Roman Catholic, and equally clear that his orders can be traced to the apostles, and that the members of his Church adhere to the faith which Christ gave us through the apostles. Orthodox priests need to clearly state which jurisdiction they serve. Those from small communions not generally recognized by other larger Orthodox bodies need to make this clear, while also pointing out that their claim to Orthodoxy is based upon their adherence to the common faith held by all who choose to be known as Orthodox.

11. No priest may seek secular employment without written permission from his bishop.

12. The priest is the spiritual father of his parish; every member shall respect him as though he were their own father. A priest is called by the name "Father" to remind him that he should treat his parishioners as a father treats his children: with love and patience.

13.   The priest, by virtue of his calling, is the presiding officer of the congregation, and an ex-officio member of the governing body of every parish organization. He must take an active part with the Parish Council in all that pertains to the financial affairs of the parish. He must not, however, be treasurer of the parish. The treasurer of every parish shall be a lay person.

14.   The priest, or a representative designated by him, shall be the presiding officer at the annual meeting of the membership of the parish, as well as all special meetings.

15.   The priest, as spiritual father, should visit every sick parishioner immediately upon learning that he or she is ill. It is the duty of every parishioner to keep the priest informed about parishioners who are hospitalized or are ill at home.

16.   A priest must maintain a church school to teach the youth of his parish the doctrines, principles, laws, and ritual of the Church. A layman should be superintendent of the church school, but the pastor is the spiritual advisor and director. Teachers shall be instructed to answer every religious question put to them by their pupils. When they are unable to answer, the pastor should be called so that he may give the appropriate answers.

17.   Whenever possible there should be a parish choir with a competent choir director. The music and hymns are an integral part of church life and should reflect the theology and practice of the Church. The pastor must give direction concerning the choice of music at all services. Secular music should not intrude in the liturgy, or at funerals and weddings.

18.   Whenever a priest is about to visit another city in which there is a priest or a parish of his jurisdiction,

the visiting priest must write the resident priest regarding his visit, and upon arrival must visit and/or call the resident priest.

19. No priest is permitted to accept an invitation to a liturgical service from another parish which has a canonical pastor, unless the invitation is issued by the pastor of the inviting parish. Any priest who violates this rule shall be dealt with by his bishop according to the Sacred Canons.

20. No layman shall set a date or time for any liturgical service without the knowledge and approval of his pastor. No layman shall have the right to invite any priest, other than his pastor, to any liturgical service; all such invitations must be made through the pastor of the parish.

21. In all inter-faith or ecumenical activities the priest shall exercise charity and discretion. He is there as a representative of Jesus Christ and as an expression of Christ's love for people of every faith. He must avoid giving the impression that there exists an inter-communion, if in fact no formal inter-communion exists.

22. Every jurisdiction requires its priests to fill out regular report forms to the bishop. In some jurisdictions there may seem to be far too many reports required, in others too few. If the bishop is to properly do his job, he needs not only to have information from the parishes, but also needs to be given this information in an orderly fashion. Even though a priest may have spoke personally with the bishop only a short time ago, he needs to complete the reports and return them to the bishop as soon as they are received. Failure to complete and return the annual report must be reported to the next meeting of the synod, and no priest shall receive his clergy card unless all

reports due to his bishop have been received in a timely manner.

II.

THE DIVINE SERVICES

1. In order to perform any divine service, a priest must be canonically ordained, must not have been laicized by his bishop, nor unqualified by his sins or lack of preparation.

2. Unless prevented by secular work needed to earn a livelihood, or by more pressing spiritual duties, a priest shall offer the Holy Mass in a church or an oratory daily.

3. The celebrants of a liturgical service must be fully vested. It is the office that must be seen and not the sartorial splendor of the individual liturgist.

4. There must be no additions to, or deletions from, the approved text of any divine service. If the Tridentine Mass is celebrated, it is to be celebrated in all parishes, everywhere and at all times in the same manner and with the identical text. The same applies to all of the approved liturgies, whether *The Liturgy of St. John Chrysostom*, *The Christ Catholic Mass*, etc.

5. The functions of the subdeacon are as follows:

    a. He may act as server and acolyte.
    b. He may read the Epistle Lesson.

6. The functions of the deacon are as follows:

a. He may read the Gospel Lesson.
b. He may offer the people the Host and the wine.
c. He may celebrate a pre-sanctified Mass.

When the deacon goes to the Church or other place where the Mass is to be celebrated, he must transport the elements in sacred vessels.

7. The jurisdiction determines at its synod whether the host at Mass is to be leavened or unleavened. The wine *must* be made of grapes and *ought* to be red.

8. The Mass must be celebrated on a consecrated antimins or altar stone.

9. The altar must be covered with clean covers. The priest shall see to it that the sanctuary and all of its contents are kept clean at all times.

10. It is prohibited to keep anything on the altar but the tabernacle, Bibles, antimins, candlesticks, vases with flowers, offering plates, and service books.

11. The priest shall see that the sexton is performing his duties properly, *e.g.*, cleaning the church.

12. The priest must see that the deacon is performing his duties properly, *e.g.*, preparing the altar for Mass, and cleansing the altar, the sacred vessels, and the altar linens.

III.

SACRAMENTS OF PENANCE/ CONFESSION AND COMMUNION

1.   The priest as spiritual father is "Guardian of the Chalice," and must encourage the faithful to receive Communion regularly and to prepare themselves properly to receive it. This means that they must offer a sincere confession before receiving the sacrament. Confession may be private or be a public confession preceding the Mass proper. What matters is that confession be sincerely offered. Latecomers to Mass who have not made their confession nor received absolution must refrain from taking communion until such time as they can participate in public or private confession before receiving communion. The priest must bring communion to those who are shut-in, incarcerated, or who have been hospitalized. He must not, however, set himself up as a judge concerning who is worthy to receive Holy Communion. He must issue warnings from time to time concerning the judgment that comes to those who receive unworthily.

2.   The Sacrament of Penance and Reconciliation is part of every Mass. The public confession therein is sufficient preparation for Communion. However, there are many who are troubled by their sins, and may prefer to confess privately before a priest and receive his counsel. The priest should be in the church an hour before Mass to hear the confessions of all who seek comfort and absolution. Wherever possible, the parish should provide confessional

booths for those who prefer anonymity when making their confession.

3. The seal of the confession is absolute. A priest may not reveal anything heard under the seal of confession. He shall not reveal what he has heard to a private person or to an officer of the court. If necessary, he will suffer fines, imprisonment, or even death before breaking the seal of confession.

4. When an act of penance is given to the confessing soul, it must be done with charity and for the purpose of helping the individual to avoid the same mistakes in the future. The practice of giving, as a penance, the recitation of the Hail Mary or the Lord's Prayer is inappropriate, because to pray is a privilege and a joy, and is not something to be associated with punishment or penance.

5. The absolution must never be given if the confessing party is not sorry for his sins and is unwilling to make restitution wherever restitution is an available option. If he has stolen, for example, he must return what was stolen or make financial payment for same. Some things have no direct restitution, such as words of hate to a loved one, but a person who is truly sorry can think of some way of bring joy where he has brought sorrow.

6. Whenever the priest encounters a penitent who brings the same problem to the confessional week after week and month after month, he should suggest that the penitent arrange to come to the pastor's study so together they may seek an answer to the problem.

IV.

THE SACRAMENT OF HOLY BAPTISM

1. Parents who come to the priest and request baptism for their children must receive counseling regarding the nature of baptism and their responsibilities to the child for whom baptism is sought.

2. Parents who are not members of the priest's jurisdiction are urged to take instruction and to become members of the Church in which the child is to be baptized. They can hardly bring up their children in a faith which they themselves do not practice.

3. Sponsors also need to be instructed regarding baptism and their responsibilities. They ought to be members of the jurisdiction which the priest serves. It is preferable that sponsors be members of the church, and, where this is not feasible because of family considerations, they should be invited as witnesses. The party also should include two other people as sponsors, *i.e.*, godparents.

4. The Baptism should be performed in the church building. Every church should have a font at the entrance of the building. In cases of urgency, baptism may be administered outside of a church building.

5. The Office for the Sacrament of Holy Baptism shall be administered in accordance with one of the canonical rites of the Catholic and Orthodox Churches.

6.   Immediately at the end of the service, the priest must enter the required information concerning the baptism in the parish record book, and shall mail the certificate to his ordinary. The ordinary shall make a copy of the baptismal record for Church headquarters, and seal and send the original document to the parents.

7.   All baptismal records are the property of the parish, and must not be removed by the priest in the event that he leaves the parish.

V.

SACRAMENT OF CONFIRMATION

1. Confirmation is a Sacrament of the Church which brings the baptized Christian into the fullness of faith. It is when a person who has been baptized as an infant reaffirms the promises which his parents and godparents made for him at his baptism. In addition to affirming his faith in Christ, the bishop asks that the confirmed may receive the gift of the Holy Spirit. The Sacrament of Confirmation is recorded in the Book of Acts, where it refers to Peter and John laying hands on those in Samaria who had not yet received the Holy Spirit. The priest must instruct those who seek confirmation that they may understand fully the faith which they are about to affirm.

2. The age of confirmation varies among the various jurisdictions and even within jurisdictions. In the Roman Catholic Church, children may be confirmed as early at the age of ten or eleven, but since Vatican Council II many parishes prefer that they wait until fourteen or even eighteen, so that they may understand with mature minds what they are about to undertake.

3. Immediately at the end of the service, the priest must enter the required information in the parish record book, and shall give the certificate to the ordinary. The ordinary shall make a copy for the Church headquarters, and seal and send the original document to the parents.

4.   All confirmation records are the property of the parish and must not be removed by the priest in the event that he leaves the parish.

VI.

THE RECEPTION OF CONVERTS

1. Those desiring admission to the Church must receive instruction sufficient to enable them to live full Christian lives and to understand the Church in which they shall give their service to God.

2. Converts who have not received Christian baptism will be received into the Church by Holy Baptism.

3. Converts who have been baptized as infants but who have not been confirmed will be received through the Sacrament of Confirmation.

4. Converts who have been confirmed in a Catholic or Orthodox Church of another communion may be received by Reaffirmation of Faith.

5. Immediately at the end of the service the priest must enter the required information in the parish record book, and mail the appropriate certificate to his ordinary, who will make a copy for the diocese and for church headquarters, and will seal and mail the original certificate to the new member.

VII.

THE SACRAMENT OF HOLY MATRIMONY

1. Marriage is a Holy Estate ordained by God and held to be a lifetime commitment. A priest who has before him a couple seeking to be married in the Church must adhere to the church's teachings regarding marriage. He must abide by the canons of the church, and, when in doubt, must consult his bishop and abide by his ruling.

2. Marriages prohibited by the church may not be performed in the church building nor by the priest, nor can the church be used by another denomination for weddings, unless the denomination has the same teachings as the priest's own jurisdiction.

3. The Sacrament of Marriage must be administered in a church building and not in a private home, in a rectory, or in any secular building or place. If necessity requires that the marriage service take place outside of a church building, a written dispensation must be requested from the bishop. Garden weddings are for those who belong to churches which worship the Great Pumpkin.

4. The marriage service takes place during Mass, and Holy Communion must be offered to all members of the Church and not just the wedding party. Holy Communion is always the function of the whole church.

5. Before performing a marriage, the priest must ascertain that a civil license has been issued to the cou-

ple, and he must comply with the civil regulations regarding marriage which are in force in his state or province. No marriage is permitted which does not meet the requirements of the official law of the local civil authorities. *However, God's law always takes precedence over civil law.*

6.   A priest is not allowed to officiate at any wedding of many grooms and brides at the same time (although a double wedding is permitted), or at any wedding that may be regarded as a stunt wedding, *i.e.*, with the bride and groom on skis, on horseback, etc.

7.   Sacred music is appropriate for sacred occasions. Secular music is unsuitable in church. "Power of Love," "I Cross My Heart," and "When I Fall in Love" are fine for the wedding reception, but have no place in official church services.

8.   After the marriage service, the priest must record all of the information in the parish record book, and shall mail copies of the certificates to his ordinary. The ordinary will send a copy to church headquarters. The license having duly been completed, a copy will be sent to the state or county or provincial official designated by law.

VIII.

THE SACRAMENT OF HOLY UNCTION

1. The Sacrament should be administered to any member of the church who has fallen ill. Such anointing should be done with the appropriate prayers for this Sacrament.

2. The Sacrament of Holy Unction shall be administered to members of the Church who are dying with the appropriate prayers for this Sacrament.

IX.

THE FUNERAL SERVICE

1. Although it is permitted to have funeral service in a home, or a funeral parlor, church members should be buried from the church.

2. Regardless of where the service is held, the casket of the departed should be closed during the service. It has been customary to have the coffin open for priests and bishops as they lie in state, but it is time to reconsider this practice. Many families will desire that the casket be open before and after the service so that friends and relatives can "view" the body of the departed. Funeral customs are deeply ingrained, and while the priest may and should advise a closed casket, he ought not insist upon it.

3. Music must always be appropriate: secular songs are not permitted in church. I was present at a funeral where "Dear Hearts and Gentle People" was sung because the deceased had loved it so much. A New Orleans funeral several decades ago had the band play, because the deceased had stipulated that it be done, the song "I'll be Glad When You're Dead, You Rascal You." Once you open door to secular music, there is no telling what song will be requested.

4. The priest should offer a funeral homily that will help the mourners understand the meaning of life and show them the spiritual resources that will enable them to cope with the death of their loved one.

5. No layman is permitted to make a speech or preach at the Funeral Mass or Service.

6. A eulogy, which is defined as a "speech in praise of a person" is best omitted. For those who have lived a good life, such a speech is unnecessary, and for those who did not, it is apt to spotlight their failures. Since almost all those at the funerals know the deceased, biographies are not only unnecessary, but often cause friction because of inadvertent errors or omissions.

7. Priests of mainline Orthodox Churches are not permitted to officiate at funerals for non-Orthodox persons. By Roman Catholic canon law funeral rites may be granted to baptized members of some non-Catholic persons under special conditions and with the consent of the ordinary. As a general rule, Roman Catholic funerals are reserved for Roman Catholics. Often, Independent Anglican, Catholic, and Orthodox clergy are called upon to officiate at funerals for persons denied burial rites by the mainline churches. In most independent jurisdictions there are no canons to guide the priest in these situations. In cases of doubt the priest should consult his ordinary.

    The independent jurisdictions need to provide clear and precise canons to cover the many situations that arise in this area, if for no other reason than the fact that funeral customs in our society are in many respects a denial rather than a positive affirmation of our faith. Also we differ on where the emphasis should be placed. One priest tells me that "The Mass for the dead is to bring solace, comfort, and to assuage the guilt of the *deceased*." He regards the concept that the primary purpose is to provide solace, comfort, and to assuage the guilt of the survivors as one of Rome's new and incorrect attitudes.

In the absence of canons in this matter, the priest and his bishop must carefully balance the two concepts. We do not by conducting the funeral service appear to imply that someone died in the faith when he did not. Having been asked to conduct funerals for persons who in their lifetime seldom or never entered a church, I offer the following poem which appeared in a church bulletin many years ago.

Whenever I pass a church,
I enter and pray a minute.
So that when at last, I'm carried in,
The Lord won't ask, "Who is it?"

But we must keep in mind that the survivors may not be strangers to God and are seeking help in their sorrow. Others, who seldom give thought to God and to the question of eternity, are more receptive to what the Scriptures and the Church have to offer than is normal in their lives. A compassionate and charitable handling of the situation can win some of the mourners to Christ and His Church. Many have been further estranged from the Church because the priest did not show compassion. The priest must seek to bring to all the comfort that the Gospel offers.

8. Immediately after the service the priest will enter the information in the appropriate register, and send the information to his ordinary so that he may have an opportunity to express his condolences.

X.

SOME PRIESTLY DISCIPLINES

1. A priest is called to preach the gospel of Christ. The best preaching is by example. A priest shall live a life of example. A priest shall live a life of obedience to Christ, Sacred Scripture, Holy Tradition, and the Canons of the Church.

2. A priest shall be obedient to the bishop. When he asks the bishop for direction on a question of marriage or funerals or any other priestly act, he is asking the bishop as the repository of faith. It then becomes mandatory that he follow the bishop's direction. Further, he will not at any time fail to consult the bishop because he knows the bishop will make a ruling with which he personally does not agree.

3. A priest must be an example to his flock through frequent prayer. He shall practice that which he preaches and encourage his congregation to follow not his example, but the example of Jesus Christ.

4. A priest must not use his pulpit for the promotion of any political cause or party. That does not mean that he must be silent on moral issues simply because they have become political issues as well. One does not remain silent for fear of meddling in the affairs of state when people are taken to concentration camps. Some affairs of state need to be challenged in the Name of God.

5.   A priest must not absent himself from Holy Communion on any Sunday without good and sufficient reason.

6.   A priest must exercise dignity and sobriety in conduct, personal appearance, and of dress. Ear rings are not to be worn.

7.   A priest must maintain a high profile in the secular world. He should wear clericals unless he is engaged in a secular job. Many people have taken their first step toward God and His church by approaching a priest whom they encountered by chance, but recognized his calling by his clerical attire. If nothing else, his attire reminds many that God's servants are in the world, are many, and are readily available.

8.   A priest must be a good steward of his resources. He needs to be careful with the use of credit. He must keep his accounts with local merchants current, and must not leave a parish without paying all accounts owing in full.

9.   A priest, even though he may be wealthy, must live a simple life. Neither his home, nor his auto, nor his dress should ever be ostentatious. It is not necessary to deprive his family of necessities or to appear to be parsimonious. He must simply be a good steward, providing for his family's needs, but never indulging himself or his family in a material show.

10.   A priest while serving at the altar must never wear more than one ring on each hand.

11.   A priest should choose a confessor and avail himself of the Sacrament of Penance at least once a month.

12.   A priest who has an active parish has to give a great deal of himself. He must be careful that he does not

attempt to do the work of God, but rather he should strive to bring his people to God, so that together they may do Godly work. Whenever a parishioner brings his problems to the priest's study, the priest should make it known that ultimately the problem must be brought to Christ. Further, he must set the example by taking his own problems to Christ. To aid him in keeping this focus, it is suggested that every priest attend at least one retreat a year, in order to keep his own house in order.

13. A priest has a right to the Canonical Courts of the Church.

XI.

UNASSIGNED AND NON-PAROCHIAL CLERGY

1. All spiritual implications of *The Priest's Handbook* apply to assigned as well as to unassigned and non-parochial clergy.

2. Clergy on leave-of-absence may not serve in any parish without the express permission of their ordinary.

XII.

REGARDING VISITS BY THE BISHOP

In most independent jurisdictions the bishop serves without salary, and cannot visit every parish as often as he might wish. However, your bishop will try to visit the parish as often as he has time and funds to do so. Anyone who feels his parish has not been visited sufficiently should petition the bishop in writing. Until he has done so, he has no grievance and shall be silent on the subject.

XIII.

PAROCHIAL FINANCIAL OBLIGATION TO THE DIOCESE

1. Each parish is required to forward to the diocese a portion (in many jurisdictions, a tithe) of all parish income. The tithe, or portion, should be paid from parish income and not by the priest or any one layman, or group of laymen.

2. Each parish is expected to support the denominational publication through individual subscriptions of its members. Contributions from parish funds are appreciated but do not have the same value as individual subscriptions. Subscribers tend to read the publication more thoroughly than those who do not subscribe.

3. From time to time, the priest must call attention to special fund raising drives from the diocese or from church headquarters. The Church tries to keep these at a minimum, but also emphasizes that that charity is one of the hallmarks of a Christian. Hence, we should bring to our people the opportunity of giving, but allow each member to determine what he is able and led by God to give.

XIV.

DEANERIES

1. Wherever parishes are close enough to form a deanery, the bishop shall define the geographic boundaries of same deanery.

2. The membership of a deanery shall consist of all priests and deacons under the jurisdiction of the Church serving or residing within the boundaries of the deanery. All retired priests under the canonical jurisdiction of the Church within the geographic boundaries of the deanery shall be invited to participate in all meetings and activities of the deanery.

    The dean is appointed by the bishop and serves at his pleasure. In accordance with the ancient name of the dean, "visitor," he shall be expected to fulfill certain responsibilities, namely:

3. He shall visit the parishes and missions of the deanery, at least twice a year.

4. He shall oversee the activities and behavior of the clergy within his deanery.

5. He shall make known and explain to the clergy within the deanery the bishop's program and plans for the churches within the diocese.

6. In cases of necessity, he shall give fraternal instructions and direction to the clergy of the deanery.

7. He shall care for the spiritual needs of the faithful in any parish within the deanery that is without a pas-

tor. In the case of a vacancy, he may appoint another priest within the deanery to provide the necessary care.

8. He shall care for the spiritual needs, or provide for the spiritual needs, of the faithful residing in areas of the deanery where no organized parish or mission exists. In most cases the deanery will not be so large that the work cannot be fairly divided among the pastors. The dean shall also explore the possibility of establishing new parishes within the deanery and to this end will work in close cooperation with the jurisdiction's missionary society.

9. The dean shall make full report to the ordinary of his activities and the state of the parishes within the deanery at least twice annually. In cases of special importance or urgency, he shall report immediately.

10. In cases of parochial dissension within the deanery which involves the pastor and the faithful, the dean shall endeavor to settle the dispute at both their invitations and/or by appointment by the bishop.

11. The dean may be delegated by the bishop to introduce a new pastor into a parish within the deanery and to preside at the function hosted to welcome the new pastor. In cases of testimonials for a priest leaving a pastorate, the dean may be delegated by the bishop to preside.

12. When visiting the parishes of the deanery, the dean shall see that everything is in good order in the church edifice; that it contains all things necessary for Divine Worship, that the altar and sanctuary are clean, that vestments are not worn or soiled, that the antimins is in good condition and signed by the bishop, that the Reserved Sacrament is kept as prescribed. If the dean finds fault with these things, he is to give brotherly admonition to the pastor.

13. The dean is duty-bound to see that all the clergy abide by the doctrines and canons of the Holy Church. In cases of violation, the dean shall report them to the bishop without delay.

14. The dean shall look to the spiritual and moral life of the clergy within his deanery, appointing a Father Confessor for the deanery, and arranging retreats for the deanery clergy at least once a year.

15. The membership of the deanery shall meet at least six times annually. A deanery which covers a large geographic area shall meet at least twice annually.

16. Concerns of the deanery shall be:

   a. Stimulation of the spiritual life of the faithful by arranging retreats, study groups, lectures, and meetings for the support of missions, both at home and abroad.

   b. Conformity to the authorized rubrics in the celebration of the Divine Services and Sacraments.

   c. Arranging seminars and workshops for the purpose of improving Christian education, liturgical music, and stewardship.

   d. Discussion of topics of pastoral concern, and working in close cooperation with the jurisdiction's liturgical commission and missionary society.

   e. Encouraging spiritual vocations, and working in close cooperation with the bishop and/or vocational committee.

   f. Stimulation of advanced theological studies among the clergy by holding seminars, bringing speakers to the deanery, and encouraging studies, either through local institutions or through extension courses.

g. Avoiding conflicting dates for parochial events by establishing a deanery calendar of activities.

h. Encouraging inter-parochial participation in special parish events, or events sponsored by the deanery.

i. The dean should take the initiative in making inter-faith contacts, strictly abiding by the "Ecumenical Guidelines" in this handbook and of the communion to which the dean belongs.

j. The dean must work constantly to keep before the priests of the deanery the need to witness to the faith in all areas of concern, especially through the media. Church activities tend to be underreported by the media.

k. The deanery shall have a secretary who shall take the official minutes and transmit a copy of same to the bishop.

l. All decisions and actions of the deanery shall be subject to confirmation by the bishop.

XV.

ECUMENICAL GUIDELINES

It is important that every priest believe that his own is the church that adheres most closely to the teachings which Christ has given us through the apostles. If he doesn't, he should leave and go to that jurisdiction which he sincerely believes is most true to the Gospel of Jesus Christ. Having become part of a particular jurisdiction, he also needs to be aware that there are other branches of the church which have a claim to both orthodoxy and legitimacy. Further, it is important that he have fellowship with many people who are members of jurisdictions, some of whom may have an incomplete, although not heterodox, view of the gospel. The ecumenical guidelines are intended to lay the basis on which we can come together without compromising the faith of anyone. Too often some jurisdictions lay down rules, much like three boys who get together to form a club in order to keep a fourth boy out. We need the fellowship of orthodox Christians of as many jurisdictions as is possible. We need to keep in mind that not all those who are outside of our communion are heterodox, and unfortunately, not all those who are inside our communion are orthodox. Ecumenical relations are important because they provide us with opportunities to meet other orthodox Christians who can enrich our lives and also afford us an opportunity to bring the faith to many who have not yet heard the complete gospel. We are also concerned about the disunity of the church and the many false impressions concerning such disunity. Not all disunity is evil. We cannot have fellowship with those who accept abortion. It is necessary and it is good to separate ourselves from those who do not accept Christ's teachings regarding life. But much of the disunion is a disgrace. Some of it has been brought about because of the quest for power by some church leaders. Some of it is social. A few jurisdictions remain separated because they feel Christians should belong to a particular class. Many ethnic churches find it difficult to believe that other ethnic groups have an equal grasp of the gospel. Unfortunately, many of these groups shun contact with other jurisdictions and so perpetuate their separation.

1.   Ecumenical Meetings:

A priest in almost any community will be invited to join various ministerial organizations. They range from the Council of Churches to more informal ministerial associations. Some, like the Council of Churches, often make pronouncements of a political nature or fund political organizations which are seen as having the support of the entire membership of the Council. These are often not organizations which the Holy Church should support. Many communities have resolved the problem by forming ministerial associations which meet to exchange ideas, to have informal conversations, and to share meals together. Since they avoid controversial subjects and seek to discuss those matters on which they agree, such associations are highly desirable.

2.   Ecumenical Dialogue:

The Holy Church is open to dialogue with many groups of Christians. However, it must be pointed out that we meet to discover where we have a common faith. There is no way that doctrine can be compromised. A discussion of doctrine is for the purpose of determining whether behind different historical formulae there is a common faith. When there is not, we go our separate ways in love. When we discover a common faith, we move to the next steps of cooperation, intercommunion, and eventually Church union. In the initial states of any dialogue a priest or layman must make clear that he is speaking as an individual believer, and does not speak for his jurisdiction. Only a bishop or the Holy Synod of the Church can speak to these questions authoritatively.

3.   Ecumenical Worship:

These days a great variety of interfaith services are labeled as ecumenical. They are conducted for special reasons, such as services for Thanksgiving, for Christian unity, for peace, in time of public calamity, or public mourning, etc. For fraternal reasons we ought to attend these services if we can do so without compromising our faith. We must be certain that no words or actions on our part imply intercommunion where such intercommunion does not exist. However, most "ecumenical" services are either non-liturgical or consist of amended versions of matins, vespers, morning suffrages, etc. Attire can be ordinary civil attire or cassock, surplice, and stole. A priest may attend "ecumenical" services that include women ministers or women rabbis, but may not attend services which include women who claim to be priests.

4.   Governing Bodies of Ecumenical Groups:

When invited, priests may accept positions on boards of directors of ecumenical associations. Such election or appointments must be brought to the bishop's attention.

5.　　Intercommunion:

Almost every jurisdiction has intercommunion with a number of other jurisdictions.　A priest will not participate in communion service with any jurisdiction that is not in intercommunion with the jurisdiction to which he belongs.　The only exception to the inter-communion rules, and this applies to some jurisdictions, but not to others, is the informal invitation to participate in a communion service held at an abbey or priory.　(A priest should know what the rule is within his own jurisdiction.)

6.　　Sacraments and Sacramentals:

Churches of both Catholic and Orthodox traditions recognize that they are not alone in conferring valid baptisms and performing valid wedding ceremonies. Hence, when we receive members who are validly baptized in Roman, Orthodox, Old Catholic, or even Protestant Churches, we do not confer "conditional baptism," but receive them by reaffirmation of faith, or if never confirmed, by confirmation.

A valid wedding is for life, regardless of where or by whom the ceremony was witnessed. Frequently, the priest will be asked to officiate at funerals for those who are not of his faith.　Some Orthodox Churches insist Orthodox funerals are for Orthodox only.　In no Catholic Church may the priest offer a funeral Mass except for those of the Catholic or Orthodox faith.　But most jurisdictions have provided special funeral services for the burial of those of other faiths and even for those who have died without the sign of faith.　The priest must keep in mind that he is being asked primarily to minister to the living who mourn, and his liturgy as well as his homily must be addressed to their needs.　It is an opportunity to bring healing of mind and spirit to those who mourn.

XVI.

RELATIONS WITH NON-CHRISTIANS

Something new is taking place in America. For the first time in history the nation has become multi-religious. It is estimated that if the present trend continues with influx of Asians and people from the Middle East, the majority of people who belong to a religious group will be non-Christian. We are getting close to this situation, but we have failed to take notice, because there are few Mosques, Buddhist Shrines, or Hindu Temples visible on our horizons. But they are there, and Christian priests, as well as the laity, have to decide how they are going to treat their new neighbors.

First, they should remember that everyone, regardless of faith, is a child of God.

Second, they should welcome them, and treat them with cordiality.

Third, although their worship may differ from ours, if they worship at all, in any manner, they may be ahead of many in our churches, who do not bother to pray at all to the God in whom they profess to believe.

Fourth, we are called to preach the Gospel to *all* nations. It is difficult to carry out this command which Jesus gave us if we do not mingle with people who do not, as yet, follow Him.

Cooperation with Non-Christian Groups:

Since we live in the same nation and in many of the same communities, Christians must cooperate with others and must lend a helping hand in time of trouble and to all who are in need. There will be times when we come together because of mutual problems and because of our involvement with mutual concerns. War, famine, drought, and other calamities will draw us together. Since the situation is so new, we have not had time to think through how and under what circumstances we can offer our common prayers together, but it behooves us to find a way. The priest confronted with a situation which calls for mutual prayers with God's children of a different house should place the need before his bishop and ask for his direction.

BIBLIOGRAPHY

The Catholic Priest, by Karl Pruter. San Bernardino, California: St. Willibrord's Press, 1993, 88 p.

Code of Canon Law. Latin-English Edition. Washington, DC: Canon Law Society of America, 1983, 668 p.

Parish Practice, by Paul J. Hoh. Philadelphia, PA: Muhlenberg Press, 1956, 248 p.

The Priest's Guide, prepared by the Department of Publications, The Antiochean Archdiocese of New York. Englewood, New Jersey: The Archdiocese, 1977, 72 p.

The Rudder: The Compilation of the Holy Canons by Saints Nicodemus and Agapius, translated by D. Cummings. Chicago, IL: The Orthodox Christian Educational Society, 1957, 1084 p.

The Theology of the Priesthood, by Jean Galot, S.J. San Francisco, CA: Ignatius Press, 1958, 274 p.

INDEX

non-parochial clergy, 35
Northeastern University, 63
obedience, 31
offering plates, 14
Office, 17
officer of the court, 16
Old Catholic Church, 48, 63
One Day with God (Prüter), 63
oratory, 13
ordinary, 18-19, 21, 24, 28-29, 33, 42
Orthodox Christian Educational Society, 51
Orthodox Church, 5, 8, 17, 21, 28, 48
ostentatiousness, 32
parents, 17, 19
parish choir, 9
parish income, 39
parish organization, 9
Parish Practice (Hoh), 51
parish record book, 18-21, 24, 29
parishioners, 15
parochial dissension, 42
pastor's study, 16, 33
Penance, 15-16, 32
penitent, 16
personal appearance, 32
Peter, St., 19
Philadelphia, Pennsylvania, 63
political causes, 31, 46
Poughkeepsie, New York, 63
prayer, 16, 25, 31
pre-sanctified Mass, 14
presiding officer, 9
priestly discipline, 31
The Priest's Guide (Antiochian Archdiocese), 51
The Priest's Handbook (Prüter), 5-6, 35, 44, 63
Protestant Church, 48, 63
Prüter, Bishop Karl, 63
publications, 39
rabbis, women, 47
Reaffirmation of Faith, 21, 48

ABOUT THE AUTHOR

BISHOP KARL PRÜTER was born in 1920 in Poughkeepsie, New York. Following high school there he completed undergraduate work at Boston's Northeastern University, and then earned his master's degree in divinity at the Lutheran Theological Seminary in Philadelphia. After starting his ecclesiastical career as a congregational minister, he wrote two books, the second of which, *Neo-Congregationalism*, was later revised to include a chapter relating the personal sojourn that brought him to the Old Catholic Movement.

In 1967 Bishop Prüter was consecrated bishop of Christ Catholic Church, and the church, under his leadership, has significantly influenced the entire Old Catholic Movement. He served as presiding bishop of Christ Catholic Church from 1967 to June 1991, when he then became suffragan bishop in order to have more time to devote to spiritual writing and to promoting the retreat movement. Throughout his work in the church, Bishop Prüter has conducted literally hundreds of retreats for both Protestant and Catholic groups.

Along with having written scores of religious pamphlets, Bishop Prüter has also authored eight books, among them *The Teachings of the Great Mystics, A History of the Old Catholic Church, The Priest's Handbook*, and, most recently, *One Day with God* (Borgo Press, 1991), a self-instructional guide to spiritual retreats. He currently resides in Highlandville, Missouri, where he serves the Cathedral of the Prince of Peace, which is listed in the *Guinness Book of World Records* as the planet's smallest cathedral, measuring 14 x 17 feet and seating fifteen people.